ROSIE HOLT

Beyond The Mic

Peregrine West

Copyright© 2024 Peregrine West. All rights reserved.

Except for brief quotations included in critical reviews and certain other noncommercial uses allowed by copyright law, no part of this publication may be reproduced, distributed, or transmitted in any form or by any means, including photocopying, recording, or other electronic or mechanical methods, without the publisher's prior written permission.

TABLE OF CONTENTS

FOREWORD 5

INTRODUCTION 19

CHAPTER ONE 31

   Early Life and Beginnings 31

CHAPTER TWO 40

   Breakthrough and Critical Acclaim 40

CHAPTER THREE 49

   The Writing Room 49

CHAPTER FOUR 61

   The challenges of being a woman in comedy
.... 61

CHAPTER FIVE 73

   The making of her debut special 73

CHAPTER SIX 86

    Beyond Stand-Up 86

CHAPTER SEVEN 96

    The Comedic Process 96

CHAPTER EIGHT 106

    Comedians who shaped her style 106

CHAPTER NINE 118

    The Bigger Picture 118

FOREWORD

The world of entertainment often presents us with polished personas, individuals who seem effortlessly perfect on screen or behind a microphone. Yet, beneath this veneer lies a journey marked by perseverance, resilience, and an unwavering commitment to one's craft. This is particularly true for Rosie Holt, whose story is as compelling as it is inspiring. In "Rosie Holt: Beyond the Mic," we delve into the multifaceted life of a woman who has captivated audiences with her voice, charisma, and authenticity. This foreword aims to set the stage for an exploration of her remarkable career, highlighting the key moments and personal insights that have defined her journey.

Rosie Holt's name is synonymous with excellence in the world of broadcasting. Her voice, known for its distinctive timbre and warmth, has become a comforting presence for countless listeners. From her early days in local radio to her rise as a national icon, Rosie's career trajectory is a testament to her talent and dedication. Yet, her success did not come overnight. It is the result of years of hard work, continuous learning, and an unyielding passion for storytelling. As you read through the pages of this book, you will gain an understanding of the challenges she faced and the triumphs she achieved, each step contributing to the person she is today.

In addition to her professional accomplishments, Rosie Holt's personal journey is equally compelling. Balancing the demands of a high-profile career with personal life is no small feat, and Rosie's story provides valuable insights into this delicate equilibrium. Her experiences offer a candid look at the sacrifices and rewards that come with pursuing one's dreams. More than just a biography, this book is an exploration of the human spirit, showcasing how determination and resilience can lead to extraordinary achievements.

Rosie Holt's impact extends beyond her work in broadcasting. She has become a role model for aspiring broadcasters and a source of inspiration for many. Her commitment to authenticity and her ability to connect with her audience on a profound level set her apart in an industry often criticized for its superficiality. Through her story, readers will find not only a celebration of Rosie's achievements but also a source of motivation to pursue their own passions with unwavering determination.

The early years of Rosie's life were marked by a deep love for storytelling and a natural talent for communication. Growing up in a small town, she found joy in narrating stories to her friends and family, often turning mundane events into captivating tales. This early passion laid the foundation for her future career. Her journey into the world of broadcasting began with a small local radio station, where she honed her skills and discovered her unique voice. These formative years were crucial in shaping her identity as a broadcaster and set the stage for her future success.

As Rosie transitioned from local radio to national platforms, she faced numerous challenges. The competitive nature of the industry required her to continuously innovate and adapt. Despite the obstacles, Rosie's determination and talent shone through. Her ability to connect with her audience, coupled with her relentless pursuit of excellence, propelled her to new heights. Each milestone in her career, from hosting prime-time shows to conducting high-profile interviews, is a testament to her unwavering commitment to her craft.

One of the defining aspects of Rosie's career is her dedication to authenticity. In an industry where image often overshadows substance, Rosie has remained true to herself. Her genuine approach to broadcasting has endeared her to listeners and set her apart from her peers. This authenticity extends beyond her professional life into her personal interactions, where she is known for her kindness and humility. Through her story, readers will gain a deeper appreciation for the values that have guided her journey and the principles that have shaped her success.

The transition to national broadcasting brought with it a new set of challenges and opportunities. Rosie Holt's ability to adapt to the evolving landscape of media while staying true to her core values is a central theme of this book. Her innovative approach to storytelling and her commitment to providing a platform for diverse voices have made her a trailblazer in the industry. As you read about her experiences, you will gain insights into the strategies she employed to navigate the complexities of the media world and the lessons she learned along the way.

Rosie's impact on the broadcasting industry is profound. She has not only set new standards for excellence but has also inspired a new generation of broadcasters. Her story is a testament to the power of perseverance and the importance of staying true to one's passion. Through her journey, readers will find inspiration to pursue their own dreams, regardless of the obstacles they may face. Rosie's ability to overcome adversity and achieve success on her own terms serves as a powerful reminder of what is possible when one remains committed to their goals.

The personal aspect of Rosie's story is equally significant. Balancing a demanding career with personal life requires a delicate equilibrium, and Rosie's experiences provide valuable insights into this aspect of her journey. Her candid reflections on the sacrifices and rewards of her career offer readers a nuanced understanding of the realities of pursuing one's passion. Through her story, readers will gain a deeper appreciation for the complexities of balancing professional and personal aspirations and the resilience required to navigate this balance.

One of the key themes of Rosie's story is the importance of mentorship and community. Throughout her career, she has benefited from the guidance and support of mentors who recognized her potential and helped her navigate the challenges of the industry. In turn, Rosie has become a mentor to many aspiring broadcasters, offering them guidance and encouragement. Her commitment to nurturing talent and fostering a sense of community within the industry is a testament to her generosity and dedication to the craft.

As you read through the pages of this book, you will discover the pivotal moments that have defined Rosie's career. From her early days in local radio to her rise as a national icon, each chapter offers a glimpse into the experiences that have shaped her journey. Her story is a celebration of resilience, authenticity, and the power of storytelling. Through her experiences, readers will find inspiration to pursue their own dreams with passion and determination.

Rosie Holt's story is not just about her achievements but also about the values and principles that have guided her journey. Her commitment to authenticity, her dedication to excellence, and her passion for storytelling have made her a beloved figure in the broadcasting world. This book offers readers a rare opportunity to gain insights into the life of a remarkable woman who has made a significant impact on the industry and inspired countless individuals along the way.

Rosie Holt: Beyond the Mic" is more than just a biography; it is a testament to the power of perseverance, authenticity, and the human spirit. Rosie's journey is a source of inspiration for anyone pursuing their dreams, reminding us that success is not defined by the obstacles we face but by how we overcome them. As you embark on this journey through the pages of her life, may you find motivation to pursue your own passions with the same unwavering determination and authenticity that have defined Rosie Holt's remarkable career.

INTRODUCTION

The world of broadcasting is a realm of fleeting fame and relentless competition, where only the truly exceptional can leave an indelible mark. Rosie Holt is one such individual, whose journey from a small-town enthusiast to a national broadcasting icon is nothing short of extraordinary. This introduction sets the stage for an in-depth exploration of her life, her career, and the values that have propelled her to the pinnacle of her profession. "Rosie Holt: Beyond the Mic" offers a comprehensive look at the woman behind the voice, revealing the determination, resilience, and authenticity that define her story.

From the very beginning, Rosie Holt's path was marked by a profound love for storytelling and a natural ability to connect with others. Growing up in a modest household, she found solace and joy in narrating stories to her friends and family. Her early fascination with the power of words and the ability to engage an audience set the foundation for her future career. This book begins with a look at her formative years, where her passion for communication was nurtured and developed.

Rosie's entry into the world of broadcasting was not a straightforward journey. It was filled with challenges, setbacks, and moments of self-doubt. Her initial foray into local radio was a critical period of learning and growth. In these early years, she faced the daunting task of finding her unique voice in an industry saturated with talent. Her perseverance and unwavering commitment to her craft during this period laid the groundwork for her future success. This book details her early struggles and triumphs, providing readers with a behind-the-scenes look at the making of a broadcasting star.

Transitioning from local radio to national platforms was a significant milestone in Rosie's career. It required not only talent but also the ability to adapt to a rapidly changing media landscape. Her innovative approach to broadcasting and her keen understanding of her audience's needs set her apart from her peers. This section of the book explores the strategies and decisions that defined this crucial phase of her career. It highlights her ability to balance creativity with professionalism, ensuring her relevance and appeal in an increasingly competitive industry.

One of the defining characteristics of Rosie's career is her dedication to authenticity. In an industry often criticized for its superficiality, Rosie has remained steadfast in her commitment to being genuine and true to herself. Her authenticity has resonated deeply with her audience, creating a bond of trust and loyalty that has endured throughout her career. This book delves into the importance of authenticity in Rosie's journey, illustrating how it has been a cornerstone of her success.

Rosie Holt's impact extends beyond her professional achievements. She has become a role model for aspiring broadcasters, demonstrating that success is attainable through hard work, dedication, and a commitment to one's values. Her willingness to mentor and support young talent is a testament to her generosity and belief in the power of community. This introduction outlines her contributions to the industry, both as a trailblazer and a mentor, highlighting the ways in which she has inspired and guided the next generation of broadcasters.

Balancing a high-profile career with personal life is a complex and often challenging endeavor. Rosie Holt's experiences in this regard offer valuable insights into the realities of maintaining equilibrium between professional aspirations and personal well-being. This book provides an intimate look at her personal journey, exploring the sacrifices and rewards that come with pursuing one's dreams. It offers readers a nuanced understanding of the delicate balance required to succeed in both realms.

Throughout her career, Rosie has faced numerous obstacles and setbacks. Her ability to overcome these challenges is a testament to her resilience and determination. This book chronicles the adversities she has encountered, from professional hurdles to personal struggles, and the ways in which she has navigated them. Her story serves as an inspiration to anyone facing difficulties in their own lives, demonstrating that perseverance and a positive mindset can lead to extraordinary outcomes.

Rosie's innovative approach to broadcasting has been a key factor in her enduring success. Her ability to stay ahead of trends and adapt to changes in the industry has ensured her relevance and appeal. This book examines the strategies she has employed to remain at the forefront of her field, from embracing new technologies to pioneering new formats. It provides readers with a comprehensive understanding of the innovation and creativity that have defined her career.

The influence of mentors and the support of a strong community have played a significant role in Rosie's journey. Throughout her career, she has benefited from the guidance of experienced professionals who recognized her potential and helped her navigate the complexities of the industry. In turn, Rosie has dedicated herself to mentoring and supporting others, creating a legacy of encouragement and empowerment. This book highlights the importance of mentorship and community in Rosie's story, illustrating how these elements have contributed to her success.

As we delve deeper into Rosie's life and career, it becomes evident that her journey is not just about personal achievements but also about the impact she has had on others. Her commitment to using her platform for positive change and her dedication to giving back to the community are central themes of this book. Through her story, readers will gain a deeper appreciation for the ways in which one individual's passion and dedication can create a ripple effect, inspiring and uplifting others along the way.

Rosie Holt's journey is a testament to the power of storytelling. Her ability to connect with her audience, to convey emotion and authenticity through her voice, has made her a beloved figure in the broadcasting world. This book explores the techniques and approaches that have made her such an effective storyteller. It provides readers with an in-depth look at the craft of broadcasting, offering valuable insights into the skills and attributes required to excel in this field.

CHAPTER ONE

Early Life and Beginnings

Rosie Holt's journey began in the vibrant, bustling city of London. Born to a modest family, Rosie's early years were shaped by the rich cultural tapestry of the city. Her parents, supportive and encouraging, nurtured her curiosity and creativity. Growing up in a diverse neighborhood, Rosie was exposed to a variety of cultures, traditions, and perspectives, all of which played a significant role in shaping her worldview.

From a young age, Rosie demonstrated a keen interest in storytelling. Whether it was through writing, performing skits, or simply entertaining her family with imaginative tales, she showed an innate ability to engage and captivate her audience. Her home was filled with books, music, and lively conversations, providing the perfect environment for a budding storyteller. This early exposure to different forms of expression laid the foundation for her future career in comedy and broadcasting.

Rosie's school years were marked by a blend of academic pursuits and extracurricular activities. She participated in school plays, debates, and any event that allowed her to perform. Her teachers often praised her for her quick wit and creative flair, qualities that would later become her trademarks. Despite the challenges of growing up in a large city, Rosie thrived, finding inspiration in the dynamic environment around her.

Rosie's first foray into comedy came during her teenage years. What began as a hobby, performing comedic sketches for friends and family, soon evolved into a serious pursuit. Inspired by British comedic legends and the vibrant comedy scene in London, Rosie decided to try her hand at stand-up comedy. Her initial performances were met with a mix of nervousness and excitement, but her natural talent quickly shone through.

Encouraged by the positive feedback, Rosie began writing her own material. Her comedy was characterized by sharp wit, clever observations, and a unique ability to connect with her audience. She drew inspiration from everyday life, turning mundane experiences into hilarious anecdotes. Her humor was relatable and authentic, resonating with a wide range of audiences.

Rosie's early comedic style was heavily influenced by the comedians she admired. She spent hours watching stand-up specials, studying the timing, delivery, and nuances that made each performance successful. This period of learning and experimentation was crucial in developing her comedic voice. She was not afraid to take risks, often testing new material and refining her act based on audience reactions.

The open mic circuit was where Rosie truly cut her teeth in comedy. These venues, scattered throughout London, provided a platform for aspiring comedians to hone their skills and gain exposure. For Rosie, these early performances were both exhilarating and daunting. The open mic scene was notoriously competitive, with each performer vying for the audience's attention and approval.

Rosie approached each gig with determination and a desire to improve. She faced her fair share of challenges, from hecklers to indifferent audiences, but each experience taught her valuable lessons. The open mic circuit was a testing ground, where she learned to handle difficult situations, refine her material, and develop her stage presence. It was here that Rosie began to build a reputation as a talented and promising comedian.

Her perseverance paid off as she started to gain recognition within the comedy community. Fellow comedians and industry professionals took notice of her unique style and natural talent. Invitations to perform at more prominent venues followed, each opportunity bringing her closer to her goal. Rosie's ability to navigate the highs and lows of the open mic circuit showcased her resilience and commitment to her craft.

As Rosie continued to perform, her confidence grew. She began to experiment with different comedic styles, pushing the boundaries of her material and exploring new themes. Her performances became more polished and sophisticated, reflecting her growth as a comedian. Each show was a step forward, a chance to refine her act and connect with her audience on a deeper level.

Rosie's journey through the open mic circuit was a formative experience. It was a period of intense learning, personal growth, and relentless pursuit of her passion. The challenges she faced and the triumphs she achieved during this time laid the foundation for her future success. Rosie's early life and beginnings in comedy are a testament to her dedication, resilience, and unwavering belief in her dreams.

CHAPTER TWO

Breakthrough and Critical Acclaim

Rosie Holt's breakthrough moment arrived with her performance at the prestigious Edinburgh Fringe Festival. Known for launching the careers of countless comedians, the Fringe was a proving ground for aspiring artists, and Rosie saw it as the perfect opportunity to make her mark. She meticulously prepared her show, "Romantic Comedian," a semi-autobiographical piece that blended her sharp wit with poignant reflections on love and relationships.

"Romantic Comedian" was a hit. The show combined Rosie's natural comedic flair with deeply personal stories, creating a unique blend of humor and vulnerability. Audiences were captivated by her ability to find humor in the complexities of romantic entanglements, and her honest, relatable approach resonated with many. Her performance at the Fringe was lauded for its originality and emotional depth, setting her apart from her contemporaries.

Rosie's time at the Edinburgh Fringe Festival was a whirlwind of performances, networking, and critical reviews. Each night, she performed to packed houses, and word of mouth quickly spread. Critics praised her innovative approach, noting how she seamlessly integrated personal narrative with comedy. "Romantic Comedian" was not just a show; it was a statement of Rosie's unique perspective and her ability to turn life's challenges into comedic gold.

The success of "Romantic Comedian" at Edinburgh did not go unnoticed. Rosie received several nominations, including the coveted Best Newcomer Award. These accolades were a testament to her talent and the impact of her work. Winning the Best Newcomer Award was a pivotal moment in her career, providing her with the recognition she had long worked for and solidifying her status as a rising star in the comedy world.

The awards and nominations opened new doors for Rosie. She was invited to perform at various high-profile events and festivals, gaining further exposure and expanding her audience. The industry began to take notice, and opportunities for television and radio appearances followed. Each accolade reinforced her credibility and showcased her as a comedian with a distinct and powerful voice.

In addition to the Best Newcomer Award, Rosie's show received critical acclaim and was nominated for other prestigious awards, including the Chortle Award and the Malcolm Hardee Award for Comic Originality. These nominations were significant, as they highlighted her innovation and originality in a highly competitive field. Each recognition served as a stepping stone, propelling her career forward and establishing her as a formidable talent.

One of the most significant aspects of Rosie Holt's breakthrough was the establishment of her unique comedic voice. Unlike many comedians who rely on formulaic jokes, Rosie's humor was rooted in personal experience and keen observation. Her ability to weave humor into everyday situations and relationships gave her comedy a relatable and authentic feel. Audiences connected with her because she spoke to the shared human experience with honesty and wit.

Rosie's comedic voice was characterized by its blend of sharp wit, emotional intelligence, and a deep understanding of human nature. She tackled topics like love, heartbreak, and the absurdities of modern life with a fresh perspective. Her material was not just funny; it was insightful and often introspective, inviting audiences to reflect while they laughed. This approach distinguished her from her peers and established her as a unique and compelling voice in comedy.

Her success at the Edinburgh Fringe and subsequent awards affirmed the strength of her comedic voice. Rosie continued to refine her style, drawing on her personal experiences and observations to create material that was both humorous and thought-provoking. Her ability to connect with audiences on an emotional level while delivering sharp, intelligent comedy became her trademark.

Rosie's journey to establishing her unique comedic voice was a process of continuous growth and self-discovery. She experimented with different styles and formats, always pushing the boundaries of what comedy could be. Her willingness to be vulnerable and authentic in her performances resonated deeply with audiences, creating a loyal following and cementing her place in the comedy world.

Rosie Holt's breakthrough with the "Romantic Comedian" show at the Edinburgh Fringe Festival marked a turning point in her career. The critical acclaim, nominations, and awards she received were a testament to her talent and the originality of her work. More importantly, she established a unique comedic voice that set her apart in the industry. Rosie's journey from aspiring comedian to critically acclaimed performer is a story of perseverance, innovation, and the power of staying true to oneself.

CHAPTER THREE

The Writing Room

Rosie Holt's rise in the comedy world brought her opportunities to collaborate with some of the industry's most respected figures. These collaborations were more than just professional engagements; they were learning experiences that significantly influenced her growth as a comedian and writer. Working alongside established comedy greats allowed Rosie to hone her craft, absorb diverse comedic styles, and contribute to high-profile projects.

One of her first major collaborations was with the legendary comedian and writer, John Cleese. Known for his work with Monty Python, Cleese's approach to comedy was both cerebral and absurd, a combination that fascinated Rosie.

Working with Cleese on a special project, Rosie learned the importance of timing, structure, and the delicate balance between humor and narrative. This experience broadened her comedic horizons and deepened her understanding of the mechanics of comedy.

Another significant collaboration was with the celebrated duo, French and Saunders. Their influence on British comedy was immense, and their unique brand of humor resonated with Rosie's own comedic sensibilities. Contributing to one of their specials, Rosie not only brought her fresh perspective but also gained invaluable insights into sketch writing and character development. This collaboration was pivotal in enhancing her versatility and creativity as a comedy writer.

Working with these comedy giants, Rosie also formed lasting professional relationships and friendships. These connections provided her with a network of mentors and peers who offered support, advice, and opportunities. The collaborations were a testament to her talent and a recognition of her potential, validating her place in the competitive world of comedy writing.

Rosie Holt's foray into television marked another significant milestone in her career. Her ability to craft engaging and humorous content translated well to the small screen, where she quickly made a name for herself as a talented writer. Her contributions to various TV shows and specials showcased her versatility and knack for creating memorable comedic moments.

One of her earliest and most notable contributions was to the hit series "Mock the Week." Known for its sharp wit and satirical edge, the show provided Rosie with a platform to demonstrate her skills in topical humor. Writing for "Mock the Week" required a quick turnaround and the ability to address current events with a comedic twist. Rosie's ability to produce clever, relevant jokes under pressure made her a valuable asset to the writing team.

Rosie also contributed to the acclaimed sketch show "That Mitchell and Webb Look." Working with David Mitchell and Robert Webb, she helped create sketches that blended absurdity with keen social commentary. Her contributions to the show were well-received, earning praise for their originality and humor. This experience further cemented her reputation as a versatile and innovative comedy writer.

In addition to her work on series, Rosie wrote for several comedy specials, including charity events and holiday broadcasts. These specials often required a different approach, blending humor with heartfelt moments to engage a broad audience. Rosie's ability to adapt her writing style to suit different formats and tones demonstrated her range and proficiency as a comedy writer.

At the heart of Rosie Holt's success in the writing room is her mastery of the art of joke writing. Crafting a joke that lands well with an audience involves more than just a punchline; it requires an understanding of timing, delivery, and context. Rosie's jokes are known for their cleverness, relatability, and sharp wit, qualities that have become her trademark.

Rosie approaches joke writing with a methodical yet creative process. She begins with observation, drawing inspiration from everyday life, current events, and personal experiences. This observational humor is then distilled into concise, impactful jokes that resonate with audiences. Her ability to find humor in the mundane and turn it into a relatable joke is a testament to her keen eye and sharp mind.

Timing is another critical element of Rosie's joke writing. Whether writing for stand-up, television, or a special, she meticulously considers the timing of each joke. The setup and punchline must flow seamlessly, creating a rhythm that enhances the humor. This attention to timing is particularly important in live performances, where audience reactions can vary. Rosie's experience and intuition guide her in delivering jokes at just the right moment for maximum impact.

Rosie also emphasizes the importance of authenticity in her jokes. Her humor often reflects her personal experiences and perspectives, making it genuine and relatable. She believes that the best jokes come from a place of truth, where the audience can see a bit of themselves in the humor. This authenticity not only makes her jokes more engaging but also helps establish a connection with her audience.

The collaborative nature of the writing room also plays a significant role in Rosie's joke writing. Working with other writers, she engages in brainstorming sessions where ideas are exchanged, refined, and tested. This collaborative environment fosters creativity and allows for the development of well-rounded, polished jokes. Rosie's ability to contribute to and benefit from these collaborative processes has been instrumental in her growth as a comedy writer.

Rosie Holt's journey in the writing room is marked by fruitful collaborations, significant contributions to television, and a deep understanding of the art of joke writing. Her experiences working with comedy greats and writing for TV shows and specials have honed her skills and established her as a talented and innovative writer. Rosie's ability to craft clever, authentic jokes with perfect timing continues to define her work, making her a respected and influential figure in the world of comedy writing.

CHAPTER FOUR

The challenges of being a woman in comedy

Navigating the comedy world as a woman presents unique challenges that Rosie Holt has faced head-on throughout her career. Comedy, historically dominated by men, often subjects female comedians to biases and prejudices that their male counterparts do not encounter. Rosie's journey through this landscape has been marked by resilience, determination, and an unwavering commitment to her craft.

One of the most significant challenges Rosie encountered was the pervasive stereotype that women aren't as funny as men. This unfounded belief, deeply ingrained in the industry and among some audiences, meant that Rosie often had to work twice as hard to prove her comedic prowess. Despite her evident talent, she frequently faced skepticism and doubt from promoters, audiences, and even fellow comedians. This skepticism was not only disheartening but also a barrier to accessing opportunities that were more readily available to her male peers.

Another challenge was the limited representation and opportunities for women in comedy. For a long time, comedy line-ups and writing rooms were predominantly male, making it difficult for women to break in and make their mark. Rosie's entry into these spaces often meant being the only woman in the room, a situation that came with its own set of pressures and expectations. She had to assert herself, navigate gender biases, and challenge the status quo to carve out her space in the industry.

Sexism and harassment were also unfortunate realities of Rosie's journey. The comedy circuit, particularly in its early years, could be a hostile environment for women. Rosie experienced instances of inappropriate behavior and dismissive attitudes, which added an extra layer of difficulty to her pursuit of a successful career.

Her response to these challenges was a mix of courage, resilience, and an unshakeable belief in her talent and worth.

Despite the challenges, Rosie Holt has successfully built a loyal and enthusiastic fanbase. Her authenticity, and unique comedic voice have endeared her to audiences across the globe. Building this fanbase was not an overnight achievement but a gradual process that involved consistent effort, engagement, and a deep understanding of her audience.

Rosie's approach to building a fanbase started with her live performances. Each show was an opportunity to connect with the audience, to make them laugh, and to leave a lasting impression. Her performances were characterized by a genuine connection with the audience, where she shared personal stories and insights that resonated with people on a deeper level. This connection was the foundation upon which her fanbase was built.

Social media played a crucial role in expanding her reach. Rosie adeptly used platforms like Twitter, Instagram, and YouTube to share her content, interact with fans, and showcase her personality. Her social media presence was an extension of her live performances, where she continued to engage with her audience, share behind-the-scenes glimpses, and provide a platform for fans to connect with her and each other. This digital engagement allowed her to reach a wider audience and build a community of loyal supporters.

Rosie's commitment to authenticity also contributed to her strong fanbase. Fans appreciated her honesty, vulnerability, and the way she addressed real-life issues with humor and empathy. Whether discussing personal experiences or societal topics, Rosie's genuine approach made her relatable and trustworthy. This authenticity fostered a sense of loyalty among her fans, who saw her not just as a performer but as someone they could connect with on a personal level.

Touring has been an integral part of Rosie Holt's career, offering her the chance to connect with diverse audiences around the world. While the life of a touring comedian comes with its own set of challenges, it also provides unparalleled opportunities for growth, learning, and audience engagement.

The rigors of touring life are not to be underestimated. Constant travel, living out of suitcases, and performing in different cities night after night can be exhausting. However, Rosie embraced these challenges with enthusiasm. She saw each performance as an opportunity to bring joy to new audiences, test her material in different settings, and refine her craft. The adrenaline and excitement of performing live, coupled with the satisfaction of making people laugh, made the challenges of touring worthwhile.

Connecting with audiences on tour was a skill Rosie honed over time. Each venue, from intimate comedy clubs to large theaters, required a different approach. Rosie's ability to read the room, adapt her performance to the audience's energy, and deliver her material with perfect timing was key to her success. She understood that each audience was unique, and she tailored her performances to ensure everyone felt included and entertained.

Rosie's interactions with audiences extended beyond the stage. She made it a point to engage with fans after shows, taking the time to meet them, sign autographs, and listen to their feedback. These interactions were not just about building a fanbase but about creating genuine connections. Fans appreciated her approachability and warmth, which reinforced their loyalty and admiration for her.

Touring also exposed Rosie to different cultures, perspectives, and comedic sensibilities. Performing in various countries and cities broadened her understanding of humor and enriched her material. She incorporated these experiences into her comedy, making her performances more relatable and diverse. This global perspective not only enhanced her comedic repertoire but also made her a more versatile and inclusive performer.

Rosie Holt's journey through the comedy world has been marked by overcoming the challenges of being a woman in a male-dominated industry, building a loyal fanbase through authenticity and engagement, and mastering the art of touring and connecting with diverse audiences. Her resilience, talent, and commitment to her craft have not only established her as a respected comedian but also as a role model for aspiring performers.

CHAPTER FIVE

The making of her debut special

Rosie Holt's debut comedy special marked a significant milestone in her career, a culmination of years of hard work, perseverance, and dedication to her craft. The process of creating this special was both a challenging and rewarding experience, showcasing her growth as a comedian and solidifying her place in the comedy world.

The idea for Rosie's debut special had been brewing for some time. She wanted to create a show that encapsulated her journey, her unique comedic voice, and her personal experiences. This special would not only be a reflection of her career thus far but also a statement of her artistic vision. Rosie aimed to produce a show that was not only hilarious but also meaningful and authentic, resonating with audiences on a deeper level.

Planning the special began with writing the material. Rosie spent countless hours crafting jokes, refining stories, and structuring the show to ensure a perfect flow. She drew inspiration from her life, current events, and her observations of the world around her. Her goal was to create a cohesive narrative that blended humor with introspection, offering audiences both laughter and insight.

Work shopping the material was a critical part of the process. Rosie performed segments of her special at various comedy clubs and open mic nights, testing jokes and gauging audience reactions. This feedback was invaluable, allowing her to tweak her material and improve its delivery. Rosie's dedication to perfecting her craft was evident in the meticulous attention she paid to every detail, from timing and pacing to the emotional arc of the show.

Selecting the right venue was another crucial step. Rosie wanted a space that felt intimate yet capable of accommodating a sizable audience, creating an environment where she could connect deeply with her viewers. After scouting several locations, she chose a historic theater known for its rich acoustics and warm ambiance. This venue would provide the perfect backdrop for her special, enhancing the overall experience for both Rosie and her audience.

The production team played a vital role in bringing Rosie's vision to life. She collaborated with a talented group of directors, producers, and crew members who shared her passion for comedy and storytelling. Together, they worked on every aspect of the production, from lighting and sound design to set decoration and camera work. Their collective expertise ensured that the special would be a polished and professional representation of Rosie's comedic talent.

As the recording date approached, Rosie intensified her preparations. Rehearsals became more frequent, and she focused on fine-tuning her performance. Her commitment to delivering the best possible show was unwavering. She practiced tirelessly, ensuring that every joke landed perfectly and that her delivery was flawless. Rosie's dedication to her craft was evident in the energy and precision she brought to each rehearsal.

The night of the recording was a whirlwind of excitement and nerves. The theater was filled with an enthusiastic audience, ready to witness Rosie's debut special. As she stepped onto the stage, the culmination of her hard work and preparation became palpable. Rosie delivered her performance with confidence and charisma, captivating the audience from start to finish. The laughter and applause that filled the theater were a testament to the success of her special.

Creating her debut special was not just about showcasing Rosie Holt's comedic talent; it was also a pivotal moment in honing her craft and defining her comedic persona. The journey to this point had been marked by continuous learning, experimentation, and self-discovery.

Rosie's comedic persona was a blend of sharp wit, relatable storytelling, and a unique perspective on life. She had always been drawn to humor that reflected her personal experiences and observations, turning everyday situations into comedic gold. This authenticity was a cornerstone of her comedy, making her performances genuine and relatable.

Honing her craft involved constant practice and refinement. Rosie believed that the key to great comedy was in the details the timing of a punch line, the nuance of a facial expression, the rhythm of a joke. She spent countless hours studying other comedians, analyzing their techniques, and applying what she learned to her own work. Rosie's commitment to mastering the intricacies of comedy was a driving force behind her success.

Works hopping her material was an essential part of her process. Performing at open mics and comedy clubs allowed her to test new jokes and receive immediate feedback. This iterative process helped her refine her material, ensuring that each joke was as strong as possible. Rosie's willingness to take risks and learn from her failures was a testament to her resilience and dedication to her craft.

Rosie also sought to push the boundaries of traditional comedy by incorporating elements of storytelling and social commentary into her work. She believed that comedy could be both entertaining and thought-provoking, and she strived to create material that resonated on multiple levels. This approach not only set her apart from other comedians but also allowed her to connect with audiences in a deeper and more meaningful way.

Mentorship and collaboration played a significant role in Rosie's development as a comedian. Working with established comedians and writers provided her with valuable insights and guidance. These experiences taught her the importance of collaboration, the value of different perspectives, and the power of shared creativity. Rosie's ability to learn from her peers and mentors enriched her comedic style and broadened her horizons.

As Rosie continued to hone her craft, she remained committed to evolving and growing as a comedian. She embraced new challenges, experimented with different formats, and explored various themes in her work. This constant pursuit of excellence and innovation ensured that her comedy remained fresh, relevant, and impactful.

The making of Rosie Holt's debut special was a defining moment in her career, showcasing her talent and dedication to her craft. The process of creating the special involved meticulous planning, hard work, and collaboration, resulting in a show that captured her unique comedic voice. Through this journey, Rosie honed her craft and solidified her comedic persona, establishing herself as a formidable and innovative force in the world of comedy.

CHAPTER SIX

Beyond Stand-Up

While Rosie Holt's rise to fame is largely attributed to her stand-up comedy, her creative ambitions extend far beyond the stage.

Recognizing the importance of diversifying her talents, Rosie has ventured into various creative outlets, each offering her new ways to express herself and connect with audiences.

One of Rosie's significant forays outside stand-up has been into writing. Her knack for storytelling and sharp wit found a natural home in scripting and screenwriting. Rosie co-wrote several web series and short films, blending humor with poignant narratives. This medium allowed her to explore different storytelling techniques and collaborate with other creatives in the industry. The success of these projects demonstrated Rosie's versatility and her ability to adapt her comedic voice to different formats.

Rosie also ventured into podcasting, creating a platform where she could engage in deeper conversations and explore topics beyond the scope of her stand-up routines. Her podcast, featuring interviews with fellow comedians, writers, and public figures, quickly gained popularity. The format allowed Rosie to showcase her curiosity, intelligence, and humor in a more relaxed and intimate setting. It provided her with an opportunity to connect with her audience on a different level, discussing everything from the intricacies of comedy to broader societal issues.

In addition to writing and podcasting, Rosie expanded her presence in television. Her appearances on various talk shows, panel shows, and sitcoms showcased her comedic talent to a wider audience. Rosie's role as a recurring guest on popular shows like "QI" and "Have I Got News for You" highlighted her quick wit and ability to improvise. These appearances not only bolstered her public profile but also demonstrated her versatility as a performer.

Social media has been another significant creative outlet for Rosie. Platforms like Twitter, Instagram, and TikTok have allowed her to share short, impactful content with a global audience. Her clever and often satirical posts resonate with a broad range of followers, helping her to stay relevant and engaged with contemporary issues. Rosie's adept use of social media has been instrumental in maintaining her connection with fans and reaching new audiences.

Looking ahead, Rosie Holt's creative ambitions continue to expand, with several potential future projects on the horizon. These projects reflect her desire to push the boundaries of her craft and explore new territories in comedy and beyond.

One exciting prospect is the development of a feature film. Building on her experience with short films and web series, Rosie is working on a screenplay for a comedy-drama that combines her trademark humor with deeper emotional narratives. This project aims to showcase her growth as a writer and storyteller, offering audiences a more comprehensive view of her creative capabilities. The film, centered around the complexities of modern relationships, promises to be both hilarious and heartwarming.

Rosie is also considering a return to the stage, but in a different capacity. She has expressed interest in creating a one-woman theater show, blending elements of stand-up, storytelling, and performance art. This new format would allow her to experiment with different styles of comedy and performance, providing a unique and immersive experience for her audience. The show would explore themes of identity, resilience, and the human condition, reflecting Rosie's growth and maturity as an artist.

Television remains a significant area of interest for Rosie. She is in talks to develop a sitcom based on her own experiences as a comedian. The show, infused with her distinct humor and sharp observations, aims to provide an insider's look at the comedy world while addressing broader social themes. This project represents an exciting opportunity for Rosie to bring her comedic vision to the small screen in a more sustained and impactful way.

Beyond these specific projects, Rosie is committed to continuing her podcast and exploring new topics and formats. She plans to invite a diverse range of guests, including authors, activists, and other creatives, to discuss their work and perspectives. This expansion reflects Rosie's belief in the power of conversation and her desire to use her platform to amplify different voices and ideas.

Rosie also aims to further her involvement in advocacy and social issues. She has been an outspoken supporter of various causes, including gender equality, mental health awareness, and climate change. Integrating these themes into her work, whether through comedy, writing, or public speaking, allows Rosie to use her influence for positive change. She is exploring opportunities to create content that not only entertains but also educates and inspires action.

Rosie Holt's journey beyond stand-up comedy is a testament to her creativity, ambition, and versatility. By exploring other creative outlets and developing potential future projects, she continues to push the boundaries of her craft and engage with audiences in new and meaningful ways. Whether through writing, podcasting, television, or advocacy, Rosie's commitment to her art and her desire to make a positive impact remain at the forefront of her endeavors.

CHAPTER SEVEN

The Comedic Process

The comedic process of developing new material is a meticulous and creative endeavor, one that Rosie Holt approaches with both discipline and spontaneity. This chapter delves into the intricate process that Rosie employs to craft her sharp, relatable, and consistently hilarious content. Her method involves a blend of observation, experimentation, and refinement, each step crucial to shaping her unique comedic voice.

Rosie's journey of developing new material often begins with keen observation. She finds humor in the mundane and draws inspiration from everyday experiences. Whether it's a conversation overheard at a café, a bizarre news story, or a personal mishap, Rosie has a knack for identifying the comedic potential in a wide array of situations. This observational skill is a foundational element of her comedic process, allowing her to create content that resonates with audiences because it reflects shared, familiar experiences.

In addition to everyday occurrences, Rosie stays informed about current events and societal trends. This awareness allows her to incorporate topical humor into her routines, adding a layer of relevance and immediacy to her comedy. She regularly reads newspapers, watches news programs, and engages with social media to stay updated on what's happening in the world. This habit not only fuels her creativity but also ensures that her material is timely and poignant.

Once she identifies a potential source of humor, Rosie moves into the brainstorming phase. This stage involves generating a plethora of ideas, allowing her creativity to flow without immediate judgment or censorship. She jots down thoughts, jokes, and scenarios in a notebook, creating a repository of raw material that she can later refine.

During brainstorming sessions, Rosie often collaborates with fellow comedians and writers.

These collaborative efforts provide a space for bouncing ideas off one another, testing jokes, and receiving instant feedback. The dynamic exchange of ideas helps Rosie refine her concepts and discover new comedic angles. This collaborative spirit is a vital part of her process, as it brings diverse perspectives and sparks creativity.

With a pool of ideas at her disposal, Rosie moves on to writing and structuring her material. This phase is where the raw, spontaneous thoughts from brainstorming are shaped into coherent, polished routines. Rosie meticulously crafts her jokes, paying close attention to word choice, timing, and rhythm. Each line is carefully constructed to maximize its comedic impact, ensuring that the punch line lands effectively.

Structuring the material involves organizing the jokes into a logical and engaging sequence. Rosie considers the flow of her performance, aiming to build momentum and maintain the audience's interest throughout. She often starts with a strong opener to grab attention, follows with a mix of shorter and longer bits to vary the pacing, and finishes with a powerful closer that leaves a lasting impression. This strategic structuring is crucial for delivering a memorable and impactful performance.

The next step in Rosie's process is testing her material in front of live audiences. This stage is critical, as it provides real-time feedback that helps her gauge the effectiveness of her jokes. Rosie frequents open mic nights and comedy clubs, where she performs new bits and observes audience reactions. The immediate response from the crowd is invaluable, revealing which jokes resonate and which ones need reworking.

Based on this feedback, Rosie enters a cycle of refinement. She tweaks her material, adjusting timing, delivery, and phrasing to enhance its comedic value. This iterative process can involve multiple rounds of testing and editing, as Rosie strives to perfect each joke. Her willingness to continuously refine her material is a testament to her dedication and commitment to excellence in comedy.

In addition to live audience feedback, Rosie values input from trusted peers and mentors. She often shares her work with fellow comedians, writers, and directors, seeking their perspectives and suggestions. This external feedback is crucial for gaining new insights and improving her material. Rosie is open to constructive criticism and uses it as a tool for growth, always aiming to elevate her comedy to new heights.

Once her material is honed and polished, Rosie moves into the rehearsal phase. She practices her routines extensively, focusing on delivery, timing, and stage presence. Rehearsals help her internalize the material, ensuring that her performance is smooth and confident. Rosie pays attention to every detail, from her gestures and expressions to her pacing and pauses. This thorough preparation is essential for delivering a seamless and engaging performance.

Finally, Rosie brings her material to the stage. The performance is the culmination of her comedic process, where all the observation, brainstorming, writing, testing, and rehearsing come together. On stage, Rosie's goal is to connect with the audience, evoke laughter, and create a memorable experience. Her ability to engage and entertain stems from her rigorous preparation and deep understanding of her craft.

Developing new material is a multifaceted process that requires creativity, discipline, and a keen understanding of comedy. For Rosie Holt, this process involves observing the world around her, generating ideas, writing and structuring jokes, testing and refining material, incorporating feedback, and rehearsing extensively. Each step is crucial in shaping her unique comedic voice and delivering performances that resonate with audiences.

CHAPTER EIGHT

Comedians who shaped her style

Rosie Holt's comedic style is a product of her unique perspective and the influence of several prominent comedians who have left an indelible mark on her craft. Growing up in the UK, Rosie was immersed in a rich comedy tradition that featured a diverse array of styles, from the sharp wit of satire to the physical humor of slapstick. This chapter explores the comedians who have shaped Rosie's comedic voice and the broader UK comedy landscape that provided the backdrop for her development.

One of the most significant influences on Rosie Holt's comedy is the late Victoria Wood. Wood's ability to blend humor with poignant social commentary resonated deeply with Rosie. Known for her sharp observational comedy, musical parodies, and memorable characters, Wood's work often highlighted the quirks of British life with warmth and wit. Rosie admired Wood's skill in making the mundane hilariously relatable and her talent for creating multi-dimensional characters. This influence is evident in Rosie's own approach to comedy, where she often draws on everyday experiences to connect with her audience.

The legendary Joan Rivers also played a pivotal role in shaping Rosie's comedic style. Rivers' fearless approach to comedy, her quick wit, and her willingness to tackle taboo subjects inspired Rosie to be bold and unapologetic in her own performances. Joan Rivers broke down barriers for women in comedy, and her trailblazing career demonstrated the power of resilience and authenticity. Rosie adopted Rivers' fearless attitude, striving to push boundaries and challenge societal norms through her humor.

The comedic duo of Dawn French and Jennifer Saunders provided another layer of influence for Rosie. Their groundbreaking show, "French and Saunders," combined absurdity, satire, and character-driven humor, showcasing their versatility and creativity. Rosie was particularly inspired by their ability to seamlessly switch between different comedic styles and their penchant for parody. The duo's dynamic performances and their ability to create strong, memorable characters left a lasting impact on Rosie's comedic approach.

Ricky Gervais' work, particularly "The Office," introduced Rosie to the art of cringe comedy and documentary-style humor. Gervais' portrayal of David Brent, a character simultaneously awkward and endearing, showcased the power of nuanced performance and subtle humor. Rosie appreciated Gervais' skill in blending comedy with uncomfortable realism, a technique she has incorporated into her own work. His influence is apparent in Rosie's ability to find humor in the awkward and the everyday, creating a sense of authenticity in her performances.

Eddie Izzard's surreal and intellectual style of comedy also influenced Rosie's development. Izzard's unique ability to weave historical references, absurdity, and personal anecdotes into his routines demonstrated the potential for comedy to be both entertaining and thought-provoking. Rosie admired Izzard's creativity and his ability to challenge traditional comedic conventions. This influence encouraged Rosie to embrace her own intellectual curiosity and incorporate a diverse range of subjects into her comedy.

The UK comedy landscape has played a crucial role in shaping Rosie Holt's comedic style. The diversity and richness of British comedy provided her with a broad palette of influences and opportunities to develop her craft.

British comedy has a long tradition of satire and political humor, from the biting wit of "Private Eye" to the clever satire of shows like "Have I Got News for You" and "The Thick of It." Growing up in this environment, Rosie developed an appreciation for the power of satire to comment on and critique society. This influence is evident in her own work, where she often uses humor to address contemporary issues and challenge the status quo.

The UK has a vibrant stand-up comedy scene, with renowned venues like The Comedy Store in London serving as breeding grounds for new talent. This thriving scene provided Rosie with numerous opportunities to hone her skills and experiment with different styles. The supportive yet competitive environment of the UK stand-up circuit helped Rosie refine her material and develop her stage presence. The culture of stand-up in the UK, characterized by its emphasis on wit and clever wordplay, is a fundamental aspect of Rosie's comedic style.

British television comedy, with its rich history of iconic shows, also influenced Rosie's development. Classics like "Monty Python's Flying Circus," "Blackadder," and "Fawlty Towers" introduced her to a wide range of comedic techniques, from absurdity and slapstick to dry humor and satire. These shows demonstrated the versatility of comedy and the importance of strong writing and character development. Rosie drew inspiration from these programs, incorporating elements of their humor into her own performances.

The alternative comedy movement of the 1980s, led by figures like Alexei Sayle and The Young Ones, challenged traditional comedic norms and introduced a more anarchic, experimental style. This movement emphasized originality, political engagement, and a rejection of mainstream conventions. Rosie was influenced by this spirit of innovation and the idea that comedy could be a powerful tool for social change. The legacy of alternative comedy encouraged her to take risks and push the boundaries of her own work.

The growing prominence of women in the UK comedy scene also had a significant impact on Rosie. Seeing female comedians like Jo Brand, Sarah Millican, and Katherine Ryan achieve success and recognition inspired Rosie to pursue her own career in comedy. These trailblazing women demonstrated that female voices were not only welcome but essential in the comedy landscape. Their success stories provided Rosie with role models and a sense of possibility, motivating her to carve out her own space in the industry.

The comedians who shaped Rosie Holt's style and the broader UK comedy landscape provided a rich tapestry of influences that have defined her comedic voice. From the observational humor of Victoria Wood to the fearless boldness of Joan Rivers, and the intellectual absurdity of Eddie Izzard, Rosie's comedy is a blend of diverse inspirations. The UK's tradition of satire, vibrant stand-up scene, iconic television comedies, and the pioneering spirit of alternative comedy all contributed to her development as a comedian.

CHAPTER NINE

The Bigger Picture

Rosie Holt's comedy is characterized by her fearless approach to tackling taboo subjects with wit and insight. From social norms to personal experiences, Rosie uses humor as a tool to explore sensitive topics in a way that is both thought-provoking and entertaining. Her ability to confront taboo subjects with humor allows her to challenge perceptions, spark dialogue, and provide a fresh perspective on complex issues.

One of Rosie's strengths is her skillful navigation of sensitive topics through clever wordplay and sharp observations. She approaches these subjects with empathy and intelligence, using humor to highlight absurdities and contradictions in society's norms. Whether it's discussing gender roles, mental health, or cultural stereotypes, Rosie's comedic approach encourages audiences to reconsider their preconceptions and see these issues from a new angle.

By addressing taboo subjects with wit, Rosie aims to demystify them and break down barriers of discomfort or misunderstanding. Her comedy invites audiences to confront difficult topics with a sense of openness and humor, creating a space for genuine reflection and discussion. Rosie believes that laughter has the power to disarm, allowing people to engage with challenging subjects in a more lighthearted and accessible way.

Laughter is a universal language that has the remarkable ability to connect people across different backgrounds and experiences. Rosie Holt harnesses the power of laughter in her comedy to forge meaningful connections with her audience. Through shared laughter, Rosie creates a sense of community and camaraderie, bringing people together in moments of joy and levity.

In her performances, Rosie uses humor to bridge divides and foster empathy. Whether performing live or through digital platforms, she seeks to create an inclusive environment where everyone can find something to laugh about. Rosie believes that laughter has the capacity to transcend differences and unite individuals in a shared experience of humor and humanity.

Moreover, Rosie understands the therapeutic value of laughter. She acknowledges that humor can provide emotional relief, alleviate stress, and offer a temporary escape from life's challenges. By infusing her comedy with positivity and optimism, Rosie aims to uplift and inspire her audience, reminding them of the healing power of laughter in difficult times.

Beyond entertainment, Rosie Holt recognizes the transformative potential of comedy as a tool for social change. Through her humorous exploration of taboo subjects and her ability to connect through laughter, Rosie hopes to encourage dialogue, promote understanding, and challenge societal norms. Her comedy serves not only as a source of amusement but also as a catalyst for reflection and meaningful engagement with important issues.

Printed in Great Britain
by Amazon